TEN

Ten

ANUNG VILAY

Courageous Creativity

Copyright © 2022 by Anung Vilay
Courageous Creativity™

All rights reserved. No part of this book may be reproduced or used in any manner without the prior written permission of the copyright owner, except for the use of brief quotation in a book review
To request permission, contact anung@courageouscreativity.co

Print: 978-1-7363008-6-2
Ebook: 978-1-7363008-7-9

The information in this book was correct at the time of publication, but the Author does not assume any liability for loss or damage caused by errors or omissions.

First Printing, 2022

Intro

It's weird to think this was 10 years in the making. I never thought I would ever share any of these. They were just little thoughts that I scratched on the side of school notes or random pieces of paper. It wasn't until a couple of years ago that I finally decided to write in one central place.
Which is pretty funny, since I usually try to be more organized. Especially with my creative stuff. But for a while, I did not give my poetry the respect it deserved. I just saw it as a quick creative outlet that would not go anywhere. Not that I didn't think it was important, but poetry and me just didn't seem to fit. It took years to see myself as creative. Then just being able to make any money from it. Not just pushing it to

the side as a partial hobby.

Also because it was a different image I saw as a poet that I could never see for myself. Though that started to change when I started adding photographer, writer, and finally author. That the image was whatever I wanted it to be. That this can be something I do all the time and can make a living from it. That any of us can live fulfilling lives.

But you decide how you want to express what's in you. It can just stay with you if that's what makes you happy. But don't hide for fear that no one will like anything you make. Your art should always be for you first. The money and recognition should be secondary, a bonus.

These poems span around ten years. It was one of the hundred times of moving that I started finding some of my old ones. Just like a journal it was a snapshot of what going on in my life and how I felt. So after I kept finding more one after the other I started to put them all together, at first to see the changes in what I wrote about and how I expressed them.

Though I did not put the poems in this book in any particular order. I made sure to not put them close to the order of when they were written. The thoughts and sentiments are what's important, not the time.

It all begins somewhere

Let it hurt

Let it wash over you over and over
Feel it in every crack it created
Let it show all the pieces it broke off
It will take your breath away
But it will not end you
After some time you'll get used to it
Then it will be less
Until the thought of it will surprise you
That is not so deep and passes quick
Let it hurt
So it won't hurt another

Time
So much to waste
Don't sit idle
Work work work
Produce something for me
What are you doing with your time?
With so much potential

I need to like who I am with you

Letting you destroy me will never save you

You told them I was difficult
You portrayed me as hard to love
All so you could elevate your character
While I had to dig mine out
Just because I let you in doesn't mean
You get to write on my pages

I am and always will be whole
Leaving pieces of me everywhere I go
But they give me parts of them to fill in

There is a fine line between having experience and
   being used

You think I've opened up
That I've shown so much
This is only surface
Puddles you splash through
The depths of me are dark
Slippery murkiness
Too easy to manipulate
Slyly directing you to other things
Discussing such deep matters
But never giving you the full answer
No one wants to touch that anger
A violence so easily roused

Keep yourself wild
Don't keep the structure of society as stone walls
Don't forget that feeling of true abandon

You cannot outrun the pain you inflict on yourself
Self-hatred
Perfectionism
Never being good enough
You'll never get away because it all started with you

Distracted by the flashing lights
But all I see is the sparkle in your eyes
All I need is for you to keep looking at me
Let them all keep turning their heads
While we stare at each other eternally

Don't let your wild be taken advantage
Don't let them discourage you from being free
That fire is what they need

My hope for you one day is to be able to
Love fiercely and freely
To not see those cracks are barriers
That someone can love you more than I could
Up close
When you're fighting battles
But also gently in the silence

Art is how we decorate space
Writing is how we decorate the mind
Music is how we decorate time

Don't trust a survivor until you know what they
had to do to survive
You won't enjoy walking with those demons

It doesn't matter if you're late
At least you showed up
The time will still pass
It's better to be a late bloomer
Then only a spectator

In order to show the depths of me
I need to rip pieces out
To bring light to them

You feel safe in your crowded places
No need to think with all the noise to drown it out
You think you pushed me into the margins
But I chose to be here
So afraid of the dark
You don't see the lush paths beyond
I embrace the dark and get to keep its secrets

Don't lose yourself trying to find how you fit with
　someone else

Your touch burns
I enjoyed every lick of the flames
Will you let it consume me
Or let it simmer across my skin?

They take pieces out of you hoping for some of your power

The lie said in truth will cut you both ways

They say I cast a spell on you
Given gold and having my way
But who's the one with the burns and scars

The same little breaks
Heals over and over
But at some point
I need to stop letting you hurt me
Or lose pieces of myself

Love is easy
The racing heart
The flush of skin
The excitement of catching a glance
That first soft touch
Soft breath
Shared memories

My gift was always for me
Not your consumption

Was it wasted time the years I loved you
When you couldn't really love me?
Yes and no
I don't regret knowing I could love this way
But I could have spread it out to others
Who could have returned

How does it taste?
When all you do is burn it
And consume it whole
Does it leave any bitterness when you
Destroy it all to fill you?

You pick at things enough
You leave nothing behind

Sometimes we can't be strong
The best we can do is not despise ourselves

Don't build a home from all your mistakes
That's a hole you'll never stop digging

Happiness may be the best revenge
But I'm petty enough to enjoy
You hitting every drop in your downfall

No emotion is bad
Its what you do with it
Jealousy to say hateful things
Or strive to do better
Anger to hurt someone
Or to defend yourself
Despair that makes you crumble
Or to make sure it never happens to someone else

To be loved by someone with such abandoned
Is both exhilarating and terrifying
To feel the poetry dance across your skin
To find clarity in all the love songs
How everything around you comes into focus
Trying to memorize every detail
Of that sweet, boundless love

It breaks your heart to be loved
When you don't love yourself
You will not believe it
Because you don't think you deserve it

How can a simple smile take my breath away
Yet never truly filled my lungs until now?

Craving something you've never had
Is a sharp kind of heartache
You don't know where to look for it
Just ache for it not being there

Some people like you miserable
It's so much easier to take from you

Is the memory of us too hurtful to remember?

Why do we worry so much about death?
We're not even living the life we have

You'll never know how my love got me to hate you

Bite your tongue, they say
Turn the other cheek
Why are you getting mad at me
For their violence?

You see me broken
Giving me sad eyes and pity
Like you didn't have a hand in it
But I get to fix me
Adding whatever I want
Into the fissures you ripped into me

Needing to rest should never be a punishment
We should not be terrified to stop moving
The sun may rise every day
And constantly shine light
But every star must die eventually

Keep that part that's always been wild
That echoes something primal
Don't let yourself be completely tamed
Let them fear that break

It is easier to stay in pieces
Then to cut yourself with your shards
Trying to put yourself back together

They'd rather you look to be whole from others
Because they can't take away something
You give to yourself

Sometimes we don't grow up but spread out

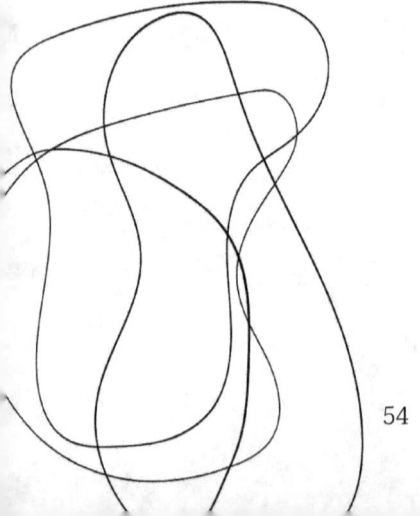

Don't Trust

We all lie
False faces in a world where no one looks
I trust no one
Least of all myself
That these pieces are not broke
Everything doesn't hurt
That I didn't tear off pieces for you
Lying that what I'm doing will ever be enough
Always my fault
Always more to take

Don't be sad for the loss of that timeline
The pain and destruction has their own beauty to it

Never wasted

You may be hurting and angry at yourself
All that time and energy
Such a waste
They strung you along, but you did all the work
Trying to build something that would last
They didn't know how to love
Mad that you couldn't do it for them
Loving someone is never a waste
No matter how unworthy they are

Just because we had history doesn't mean you
Can step in my present
You did not walk with me when I had to fill in the pieces torn off
These patchworks together I made myself
You don't get a choice to run your hand over again

Why was it left up to me to fix you?
When you hated it every step
Every unhappy moment to make better
Your worry always more important than my pain

This wisdom was hard won
Did you think knowledge was free?
You can't just observe it on the side
It needs to be experienced
Sometimes leaving you broken and bruised
But you get up and face
Sharing it so someone else doesn't have
To win it the same way

Maybe that love we're looking for doesn't send sparks
But adds comfort in the quiet moments

Stop looking for someone else
when you are lonely
You will always have you
and that is the greatest comfort

When looking back don't just think of the pain
You came back to yourself

Its never too late to change yourself
You don't stop having fun after your 20s
You're never too old to find something or someone
new to love
You are and always will be a whole person
Not everything is meant to be shared
But also be loud about what you are proud of

Letting go does not mean losing
all my memories of you

Some things you can only learn in a storm

Love

Such a fragile thing
Fragile since the smallest thing can shake it
It's not with a hard swing that breaks it
But a million little senseless cuts
Strong for all the storms it can weather
Being the only thing keeping some alive

No one should be confused about how
I should be treated by how I do it myself

Be fluent in silence

Other people's approval will never give you
Meaning or value
You should never have to earn your own love

Build from your ashes
Don't let them break you
Those cracks let the light and air in
Build the fire inside
Burn all their expectations to ashes
The forest may be burned, but it is not dead
Sprout grows with the new nutrients
Gaining substance from the bad

It use to be hard

Beginnings are always hard
Never knowing
Always new
To learn, to grow should always be hard
Just like a toddler taking their first steps
We will all stumble and fall
But as adults, we need to lose our fear of that
With practice, it gets easier
But forget that it used to be hard

We may not get what we want but what is needed

Sometimes we need the pain

We need the fire to burn the whole forest down

But life is not all truly destroyed

Something can always grow from the ashes

Risen from all the exterior places on us

What was hidden now allows light

What would you set free?

Does my strength make you uncomfortable?
My play on words leave you speechless?
Should I care what you don't like?
Put you on a pedestal when you couldn't
get up there on your own?

I still see you in the scattered wildflowers
Growing wherever you are thrown
In the fleeting scent in the lilacs
Such short-lived blooms but hard to ignore
The cherry blossoms thriving in foreign soil
Not deterred by unfamiliar surroundings

Endings and beginnings come and go
Over and over
Don't think your ending will be it for me

Go ahead
End it
Seeing your back will not be the last thing I'll see
You know I'll see more eyes
And touch more lips
Their touch will make me sigh
The memory just to torture

My hope is not delicate
Not ethereal
I built it up off the dirt
Formed it with my blood-stained hands

But loving will always be hard
It will always be hard because it has
nothing to do with you

The pain is in the waiting
For the call
To be picked
To be accepted
It can only be relieved in the now
Living with what you have

The heartache of wanting to be wanted
To be the first person you call
The hand you actually want to reach for
Someone you want to be shared
And share things with
It's not a thought for you to touch my lips
To want me in your arms
But I'll never be that for someone
Not even a second thought
The ink on the page will only hold me for so long
A substitute for the warmth of being wanted

Anger is meant to be respected
It is a direction for
A boundary stomped
A hurt brushed off
It is fuel for our action
A way to listen in
It shows us what loyal is
With no care for being nice

You being all you have in the end
should be a comfort
Not a punishment you are stuck with

You can lose yourself in the day to day
But the rain can bring you back

A day of endless sun
Grateful for the light but missing the night
But it is just the beginning of the summer
Of blessed heat and ice cream treats
Memories of carefree play and freedom
A cycle that ends too soon

I'm changing for me
Everyone else will have to rise to my level

We shape who we are
Constantly changing
Blooming where we want
Damn the concrete paths society forces onto us
My roots will slowly rip it apart

Your worth is always there
It cannot be earned
So no one can take it from you
You do not have to deserve happiness
Deserve content
Deserve rest

Just because someone else could not love you
Does not make you unlovable
I love a raging storm
But will never be able to embrace it
Does not diminish my feelings
Nor that it needs to lessen itself to receive

Leaving is easy
Once the decision is made
Pack my bags
Delete the pictures
But all I needed was a reason
No one would give me one to stay

We're all told about the explosive love
But never the calm tending one
We should crave their touch
Get excited by a kiss
But also the one we can share the quiet with
We all should have a love that makes us
Grateful to exist

You can be proud of whatever you want
Fuck the American dream
Be happy not having kids
Glad you did not get married
Proud you got a divorce
Grab at the things that bring you joy
No matter how small and insignificant
they are to others

Keep that glow of the unbothered
That inner strength that shakes others
While you tread on no path
They get trampled on the well-used road

May you reach past the horizon you see
Taste a passion you have no words for
Hear a truth that is meant for you
See every star that will grant you a wish

Your soul is boundless
But that doesn't mean we don't have boundaries

Spite is an excellent motivator

Growing into yourself is a series
Of becoming and unbecoming
Over and over again

Misery should not be relatable
I don't need to be dragged down with you

Forever is only as long as you make it
What truly can last is not always up to us

You shouldn't fear me hating you someday
But how you will be easily forgotten
That I'll never need your apology
In how little energy and emotion I will put in you
Just days of apathy until you disappear

Peace is so hard to achieve
Because it is so simple
We always try to complicate things
Adding things left and right
Instead of just having less

Joy and hope can only be kept if
Respect and dignity come along

Being lost does not negate being worthy
You can still be happy while you are searching

There is strength in your kindness
Beauty in the break
True happiness in contentment
Yet we fear all that quiet

You are allowed to let the heavy be too much
To not rise today and face the day
To let the tears drown you for a while
Scream if you must
Until your voice cracks
We can't be strong every day
We shouldn't have to fight every battle

Tend to your heart
Because no one will be able to do it fully
A parent's love can only cradle you so much
A friend can only guide you so far
A lover can cherish only what they see
There will be parts of you that no one will know of
But it still needs care in the safety of the dark

They teach you about the cycle of life
About growing and learning
But they leave out the wilting and dying
It is a natural cycle
Cause what goes returns to the earth
And you can grow from that anew

Let me return

Let me turn into the salt
Back into the ocean
The ember that slowly is
Consume by the flame
Worm food to become dirt
For the trees to grow
The whisper of wind
Carrying a memory
The spirit turned to
Stardust

Anung is an author of non-fiction and fantasy. And now a poet. Runs her artist business (anungvilay.com) where she shares how people can be brave enough to be more artisic and creative. Also runs Courageous Creativity whichs helps people bring creativity to their everyday lives. And shows ways that they can make money from that, either as a side hustle of business.

She is also the host of The Introvert's Bubble and I Do Wanna Fit In podcasts. Serial starter and dreamer.

She lives in Minnesota with her dog and coworker Enzo Who has won Employee of the Month for years somehow. Constantly reading, writing, and creating.

www.ingramcontent.com/pod-product-compliance
Lightning Source LLC
Chambersburg PA
CBHW072101110526
44590CB00018B/3262